GONE HOLLYWOOD

Laurence Overmire

INDELIBLE MARK PUBLISHING

Indelible Mark Publishing 2011

Copyright © 2011 by Laurence Overmire.

All rights reserved. This book, or any part thereof, may not be reproduced in any form without permission, except in the case of brief quotations embodied in critical articles and reviews.

Printed in the United States of America

Front cover photo and interior photos by Laurence Overmire

Back cover photo and page 1 photo by Nancy McDonald

Library of Congress Control Number: 2010938626

ISBN 978-0-9795398-3-1

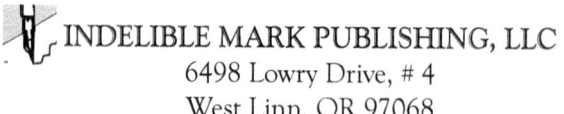

INDELIBLE MARK PUBLISHING, LLC
6498 Lowry Drive, # 4
West Linn, OR 97068
www.indeliblemarkpublishing.com

For the Survivors

Other books by Laurence Overmire

    Honor & Remembrance
        A Poetic Journey through American History

    Report From X-Star 10
        Sci-Fi Poetry

    One Immigrant's Legacy
        The Overmyer Family in America, 1751-2009

Videopoems by Laurence Overmire on YouTube

    Ode to an Endangered Species
    Viewpoint
    Beach Walk at Sunset

Contents

Members Only	1
Waiting. Outside the Gates of Paramount.	2
The Casting Director	3
Marketing and Research	4
Who Wants the Drumstick?	5
The Lost Works of Shakespeare	6
Wait For My Cue	7
Sitcom Soufflé	8
Game Show	10
Starlet	11
Gone Hollywood	12
Who Wants to be an Idiot	13
Sink Hole	14
The Angel and the Devil	15
A Supermodel in Bed	16
Do the Limbo	17
The TV Executive	18
Porn Star	20
Rabid Dog	21
Tables Turned	22
Elmer's Toon	23
Tee Vee	24
Del Usion	26
Of Traffic Jam and Toast	27
The Famous	28
Andy's Flagrant Moon	30
Waitresses	31
The Reaping	32
Move to Sedona	33
Beverly Hills Billie	34
The Face in the Tube	35
The Climb to the Top	36
The Box Office Draw	37
Hollywood Surgeon	38
Luck Be an Oscar Tonight	39
When Film Stars Collide	40
Media Mogul Genius	41
Swallowing Goldfish	42
Pundits	43
Ozzie and Harriet Got Cancelled	44
No Sunglasses	45
Ozymandias II	46
An Actor Prepared	47
Mister Successful Man	48
Face-to-Face	49
Only in Vegas	50
Down with the Ship	51
Movie Magic	52
Disneyfied	53
Mouths of Babes	54
Celluloid Lovers	55
Santa Monica Pier	56
The Envelope Please	58
Celebrity Watching	59
Silver Screen	60
Bernhardt on her Knees	61
Griffith Park Observatory	62
Close Call	64
Who Killed the Fourth Estate?	65
Colorado Dreaming	66
While Turning Off the Television	67
Winners and Losers	68
Does Anyone Remember?	69
The Hollywood Ending	70

MEMBERS ONLY

On a dark street marked "Hollywood"
   Down a dirty, refuse-laden alley
      'Neath the glow of a smog-downed moon

Limping to the door
   To knock three times in code
      Bump-ba Bump

Snake-eyes open through a throat-cut slit
   Query
      "What's the password?"

"Take no prisoners."
   Chuckle. Chuckle.
      Door unlocks.

"Come on in and join the party.
   We've been waiting for you."
      Fade to black.

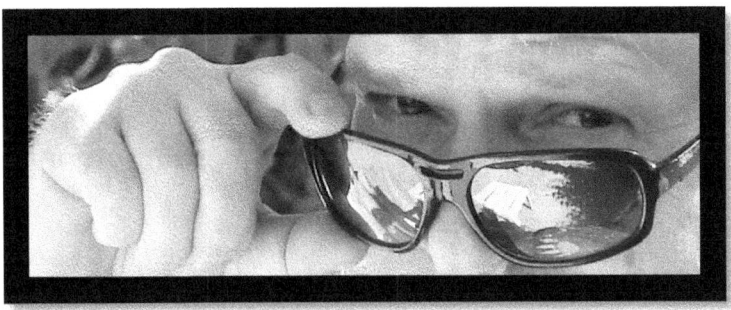

WAITING.
OUTSIDE THE GATES OF PARAMOUNT.

I'm selling my personality
Which is kind of hard to do
Because I don't have one

But it's why I'm an actor after all
Trying to find a mask
In this pile of real or imagined junk

That fits.

The Casting Director

He's the guy in the pony tail
With the sandals and no socks
A hep-hop hipster who knows with the whiff of a whim
What flavor is preferred at any given moment.
Be it chocolate or vanilla, banana or spumoni
He knows the scoop
And whips up a frothy concoction of blondes and brunettes
Talls and shorts, skinnies and fats with nuts on top.
He reads all the biz mags
Knows what sizzles and what flops
And especially who the tweenies want to see for ten or twelve bucks a pop.
No swizzle on a stick, he's an artist at what he does
A man with a vision —
Of Malibu you can shoot up your nose.
Actors call him by his first name, Chuck or Francois or
Whatever it may be
And send him postcards and flowers and candy and such
But he seldom returns their calls.
He wanted to be an actor himself once
But he couldn't take the rejection.
Now he plays his cards close to his trendy vest.
His chips are stacked like bimbos and he knows it.
He's just biding his time
Patiently waiting for the right opportunity
To cash in
And realize his lifelong dream —
To direct!
Meantime, he'll compound his assets and turn his kid into a Movie Star.
After all, his high-powered producer friend
Owes him a favor.

MARKETING AND RESEARCH

To suit
The popular taste
Of a sweet-toothed, tongue licking
Minor-minded entity called
Hollywood
All eyes fixed
On the swirling S, stroked twice
In parallel, no one thinking how the

Image

Projected like a god upon
The altar of an impressionable
Mind
Spins counter-clockwise
More to the devolution
Of a captivated ape
Than to the sapient progress
Of a higher

Species.

WHO WANTS THE DRUMSTICK?

After compromising every principle
And aesthetic value he ever had
Conforming his every idea to the
Stricture of the nefarious Bottom Line

They stuck a fork in our
Unfortunate friend
Determined he was cooked and
Brought to the table

Another well-seasoned turkey
To do the re-writes and
Completely overhaul
The script.

The Lost Works of Shakespeare

Thank God the truly wretched works of
Shakespeare
Were never produced or brought to light.
For that small piece of good fortune
The old bard must be truly grateful.

Think of it
They must have existed once
Little-known drafts of real stinkers like
"Cicero's Bathtub"
A horrid little tragedy in the Greco-Roman style
Or perhaps
"Helmut und Brunhilde"
An impossibly unfunny romantic comedy set
In a German brothel.

No. They are forever lost to our great relief.
Had they been extant, surely some high-minded
Critic, quick to make a name
Would have declared them masterpieces
And some sleazy production company
Would have turned them into
Even cheesier Movies of the Week.

Wait For My Cue

In this next shot I want
Pure bullshit
I want you to give me all you've got
Push every emotional button
Laugh, cry, rage
SCREAM until your head spins around
And a squinky little rubber alien thing
Pops out of your stomach.

And if that doesn't put a few dollars in our pockets
I'll give up filmmaking altogether
And go back to doing
Television.

Sitcom Soufflé

Always start with a big batch of dollars.
Pour it into the tube quickly;
No need to worry about spilling.
Speed is of the essence, time is money.

Now spoon in a generous helping of sex:
Hunks and babes with very white teeth and
Appropriately big body parts.

Add 2 cups innuendo, 4-5 tablespoons of witless
Sarcasm,
And a scoop or two of old stale jokes.
(You can get these on sale by the bushel at any local convenience store).

Mix well with impossible circumstances —
Completely devoid of intellect with no discernible
Link to reality.

Turn up the heat to high.

Whip in some popular music, some très chic clothing,
A couple of silly parents, a dotty neighbor,
And a dog or other cute animal who does tricks.

As the pablum begins to boil into a bubbly froth,
Fold in a boisterous laugh track, making sure to cover
Any and all portions of the material that are in no way
Funny or clever.

Note: For the typical soufflé, several gallons of
Laugh track may be required.

Pop your sitcom into the oven.
Bake for at least 15 minutes of fame.

When you begin to smell the profits,
Remove carefully and allow the sponsors
And network censors to taste the product,
Removing any extraneous relevance.

Voila! That's all there is to it!
Serve your masterpiece to the American Public
With an appropriate disclaimer assuming no
Responsibility for undesirable side effects related
To the consumption of your product.

GAME SHOW

Find a penny. Take a penny. Stack a penny, please.
Earn a penny. Add a penny. Stack the pennies, please.
Add a nickel. Add a dime. Stack the pennies, please.
Add a quarter. Add a dollar. Stack the pennies, please.

Save a dollar. Earn a dollar. Stack the pennies, please.
See a dollar. Take a dollar. Stack the pennies, please.
Hide a dollar. Steal a dollar. Stack the pennies, please.
Make a thousand. Take a thousand. Stack the pennies,
Please.

Get a dog. Get a wife. Stack the pennies, please.
Buy a house. Buy a car. Stack the pennies, please.
Invest a bundle. Make a bundle. Stack the pennies, please.
Have a kid. Ignore the kid. Stack the pennies, please.

Taste a million. Make a friend. Stack the pennies, please.
Hoard a million. Break a friend. Stack the pennies, please.
Divorce a wife. Take a wife. Stack the pennies, please.
Eat a million. Cheat a million. Stack the pennies, please.
Buy a soul. Sell a soul. Stack the pennies, please.

Bzzzzzzzzzz!!!! Time's up. You're dead.
Turn in your pennies, please.

Starlet

She might have been 60 or even
70, we couldn't tell

Her face was stretched and cut
So close to the bone

The make-up laid so thick
A wig to hide

The barren scar of scalp
Her fingers

Reaching back to a long lost past when
Beauty was an ardent player

Upon life's trifling stage
And fortune, strewn across a

Primrose path, but a look and
A smile and a

Wicked toss of the head.

Gone Hollywood

He used to be a nice guy
Before he went to Hollywood.
He was a good kid
Friendly, likeable
Down to earth.
He had big dreams.
Everyone thought he would go far.
Unfortunately
No one really knows what happened
Except that
He went to Hollywood.
Now when you see him
He's much friendlier than before.
Why, he's dripping with friendliness.
He smiles too much.
He laughs too hard and
He likes to slap you on the back and
Almost knock the wind out of you.
You'd like to find out what he's thinking
What he really feels
But you can't
Because he never takes off his sunglasses.
Oh he's very successful
He drives a Mercedes
A gold Mercedes
But he gave up all those wonderful dreams he had.

Now he's an agent.

Who Wants to be an Idiot?

I do! I do!
I want to go on TV
And expose myself
For the imbecile that I am.

I want people to see me on the street and say
"Hey, that's the idiot we saw on TV!"
After all, fifteen minutes is better than nothing.

And maybe if I'm really obnoxious
They'll even give me my own sitcom.

Or at the very least
One of those weight-loss commercials
Or an in-depth interview on
Fox & Friends.

Sink Hole

He made the mistake of standing on top of
The television set.
He thought maybe he could conquer it, I guess

But instead
It swallowed him up and burped him out into an
Infomercial.

And if we don't pay $149.95
In six easy installments
We'll probably never see him again.

THE ANGEL AND THE DEVIL

The angel and the devil
Were married in his heart
They slept together and made
Impossible children
Good-natured bastards, villainous saints
And with a kiss and a smile
He'd slip a knife in your back

Tending to your wounds

With a smirk in his eye
And though you loved him like a brother
You had to let him go
The thin rope slipping from your fingers
The quicksand of his nature
Swallowing the last hope
Of something more.

A Supermodel in Bed

How many times do I have to tell you, Harry
Look. Don't touch.
You know how long it takes me to do my hair?
Hours, Harry, hours. So don't you dare mess with it.
And my nails. If you so much as chip the gloss
Why —
Well, I'd rather not think about it.
But it'll cost you —
Big time, buddy!
So just you keep your hands to yourself.
And, Harry, please I haven't got all night.
I've got to get up at 4 for a 7 a.m. shoot
So make it quick, okay.
Hey! What did I tell you about those hands? Off! Off!
Okay, good, that's over.
Now just roll over and go to sleep.
What? A cigarette?!
Do you know what cigarette smoke does to my skin?!
You're damn right we'll forget about it.
Now turn off the light.
Oh, and Harry, stay over on *your* side of the bed.
I don't want you poking me in the eye or something —
That could put me out of work for months.
And then where would you be?
Out on the street with all of your loser friends.
And none of them have ever been to Paris or Monte Carlo
And don't you forget it!
Now hush up and give Teddy Beddy a kiss.
Night-night, sweet-ums.

DO THE LIMBO

He loved her for her beauty.

She loved him for the cars, the furs
The jewelry, and the address.

Together they made a spectacularly
Shallow couple.

The perfect husband and wife team to anchor
The news on Channel 7.

THE TV EXECUTIVE

The television executive hangs by a string from a
 corporate digit
Fiddling with the twiddle of his thumb
Fantasizing of half-clad dollar bills spread provocatively
 on the sofa
So conveniently placed in the center of the room.
His finger snaps. His secretary barks.
Dogs come running out of the woodwork
Panting and licking
Ready to fetch his slippers and light his cigar.

Yes, life is a pool in the Hollywood Hills
With starlets to twinkle their charms
In tending the dangling needs of a silver-spooned ego.
The sip of a julep is oh so sweet when sucked through
 the nectar of adulation.
But alas
His time is short.

The balding butler, with just a hint of a smirk
Serves him a cell phone on a silver platter.
Holding the perilous instrument gingerly to his ear
Our TV boy is scolded by a box of laundry detergent
Who tells him that Nielsen doesn't like his numbers and
He's being banished to a subsidiary existence
In New Jersey.

Porn Star

He goes to work like the rest of us
Suit-and-tied to his paycheck
But talk about a horrible job
He's taken the optimal experience
    a life has to offer
And turned it into something
Tedious, mechanical and even
Routine
The most intimate aspects of himself
Squandered on the tawdry, unclad dalliance
Of every Tom, Dick and Judy
Used like a condom
And discarded on the vile
Indiscriminate
Trash heap of wasted
Human endeavor.

When he finally gets home to his own bed
Early in the dilapidated morning
The emptiness is shattering.

Rabid Dog

Drinks out of the toilet of life
Tattooed and pierced
Spitting images of disgust
Through rapturous ecstasy
Of bloody nose
Rock 'n Roll
Riffs of anger up and down
Open flies and unsnapped bras
Screaming groupies
Begging for mercy in cheap
Hotels, limos opening and closing
In a frenzy of deceit
Smoked glass and spectacle
Roadies to stoke the show
Agents on short fuse
Caught in tirades
Bickering dollars mounting
Back-room safes with lucrative combinations
Penthouse suites luxuriously laid
High above the grimy
Stuck-bubble gummed pavement
Discarded soda cans on
The seemy [sic] side of
Sunset Boulevard.

TABLES TURNED

It has been my privilege to clean the floors of
Some of the most famous people in the world today.

Why, I have been spit on by the very best and
Made to look like a fool in front of thousands of

The most distinguished luminaries of our time.
So if you want to fire me, go ahead.

But just remember, you and your petty little toilets
Aren't worthy of the scrubbing of a master

Like me!

Elmer's Toon

Elmer Fudd accidentally shot
A sacred cow
With his toe on the trigger
Instead of his finger

Ducks and bunnies broke into
Choruses of song
To see their cartoon world order
Turned categorically upside down

But animators are only human
Certainly not deaf to the clamor of
Anthropomorphic prejudice
That assails the hides of reason

With the quick stroke of an eraser
The ugly deed was
Parted like the red sea
And the cow resurrected

Four feet to the ground in solid gold
Television once again made
Holy (cow)
For each intolerable generation of

Imperturbable mind.

TEE VEE

Watch the Box
Blip Blip Blip Blip
Watch the Box
And lose your mind

Eat the plastic
Blip Blip Blip Blip
Shoot your Wheaties
You're feeling fine

Bogey's my baby
Blip Blip Blip Blip
His life ain't lazy
Gimme some wine

Jack my rabbit
Blip Blip Blip Blip
Hot 'n slinky sex babes
Blink me blind

Sell me some stink juice
Blip Blip Blip Blip
Eighty bucks a bottle
But it ain't no crime

I want to do the laundry
Blip Blip Blip Blip
See if Presto Cleanso
Really leaves no grime

Hey look at that dude man
Blip Blip Blip Blip
Blew his own head off
But his glasses still shine

Blip Blip Blip Blip
Blip Blip Blip Blip
Blip Blip Blip Blip
Bleep.

DEL USION

If you knew the person
   He thinks he is

You'd have to admit
   He's one very special guy.

Of Traffic Jam and Toast

Trying to get somewhere
A place I want to be
On a road I suppose will take me there

But

Stuck on the pavement
A slow roll of tires and fumes
Bumper to bumper
Trying to see why
The Fates have blocked my going

But

There is only an endless chain
Of car to car, twisting up and down
The impertinent Valley
As far as eye can see
Angry faces glare in the heat
Pounding ineffectual fists
Raging horns that bleat like sheep
Before a shearing.

THE FAMOUS

Hide

In very large boxes, wired and chained
Houdini with no escape
Magic only in the flutter of
Eyelash blinkers waiting
Outside walls
For a glimpse of something
More than ordinary.

Ducking through back doors
Body-guarded
Swanky shops on Rodeo Drive
Seen and not seen
The push and shove of
Paparazzi ubiquitously situated
To leach a cover, candid shot
In awkward moment
Compromised.

On every sidewalk corner
The glare of strangers
Unnerving in its gauche display
Like flies on cold meat
Exposed

All the while
An immaculate smile pasted on gritting teeth
Starry eyes seething behind tinted glass
A wave of a covered hand
Studded with diamonds
To drive the image

Home.

ANDY'S FLAGRANT MOON
(A Tribute to Andy Kaufman)

He did it yes he did
He mooned us
Right there in front of everyone
We thought he was being funny
That we were supposed to laugh somehow
But that wasn't it at all
The joke was on us
How long would we tolerate our own
Silliness
The absurdity of our own media-driven
Buffoonery?

What a gas he had
Wicked trickster, divine provocateur
A pock-marked lunar-tick
We just didn't get it
We are free to create
Sanity or madness, it's all the same
In the swirling dust
Of banged-out stars, moving
Deep into the unknown reaches of an infinite space
Beyond the dulling edge of an easy
Punch line.

Waitresses

Priscilla is the homely one
Late shift
Hard worker, very polite, but
Rarely sees more than 15%
From the hot-shot lawyers, big corporate boys
Who live it up raucously after hours
Dull wits ready to appease the wife with a fib

But Betty has boobs
The bouncing blonde
And when she *does* work
(Those nights when she's in the mood)
She'll rake in four or five hundred cash
Easy.

The Reaping

Little Dickie's head pushed out of the womb in 1981
A television perched on top of his crib
Sang him to sleep when his parents weren't there.

At 10, his boy blue bedroom walls were decorated
With superstar heroes, shoe-contracted millionaires
Logo-painted men
Who'd scaled the heights of fame
Crushed the competition with overpowering skill and
Ruthless ambition.

At 15, his mind was designer-labeled
Branded with a corporate calling card
A devoted follower of common taste and popular sense
An unseen desire to find himself
Driving his insatiable need
For more and more.

By the time he became Big Richard
A distinguished shark in nameless-fish infested waters
He had become his own unbecoming
Without a tear
His bladed pen sliced across the fateful piece of paper
Acquisitions compounded
Assets merged
Pockets lined
While thousands dropped from unfeeling ledgers

Their lives suspended

In an impotent
Hell.

Move to Sedona

The woman wrote a screenplay
She thought was brilliant and
Cast herself in the lead

The poor director didn't stand a chance
Crushed by the enormity of her ego

The other actors bit their tongues
Cursing their agents for getting them
Involved with such a colossal flop

Despite the setback, she persevered
Wrote a brilliant sequel, starring herself

(Good thing she was married to an unnamed
    Mogul, willing to spend the cash
        To keep his little Mrs. occupied)

New director, new cast
New facelift, new wardrobe
And a brand new marketing strategy

She was determined to be a Hollywood star!

BEVERLY HILLS BILLIE

Oh he was so attractive!

He was like a vice president or something and owned
A big house in Malibu
With like a pool and tennis courts and everything!

But then there was like all this rain
And his house like fell down into all this like mud.
That's when I like realized he was just another nerd.

So we broke up.

THE FACE IN THE TUBE

In order to eat
To keep my kids in clothing
I sell gimmicks on TV
Oh yes, I'll tell you it's the best
That nothing else will do
I'll say anything they want me to
Because they made me what I am
And you'll believe me because
You think you know me
You trust the sincerity of my smile
Yes, we all do what they want us to
Pretending we're happy doing
What we do
Pretending that we really have no choice
It's just the way it is
And always has to be
No use at all pretending
Otherwise.

The Climb to the Top

The daughter of famous parents
She changed her name to
Forge her own identity
Separate from the titanic pull of
Expectation and privilege

After struggling unrecognized for a
Couple of months
She asked Mommy and Daddy for a
Favor
Hooked her up with a top-of-the-heap agent who
Promptly

Launched her career
With the quick pull of a couple of
Strings

Now she goes on talk shows and
Tells people how hard it was —

The climb to the top.

The Box Office Draw

Looks in the mirror and sees
God, created in his own image
Little folk stretching in lines
Breaking barricades to
Worship at the altar of his
Shining shoes
A swift flourish of his pseudonym
On a crumpled piece of paper
Enough to garnish hundreds

On an open market of fools

In a trailer on the lot
Scotch loaded on the rocks
He thinks himself invincible
With the barrel in his mouth
What power to make or break
To grant
Or deny
Immortality contained in the tip
Of a twitching finger.

HOLLYWOOD SURGEON

Hey, nice sunglasses. Ray-Bans. That's a good start. But, oh, look at this. A crooked smile. That won't do. A smile must sparkle. Dazzle, in fact. The smile is like the closed window to the soul. Even the slightest ulterior motive must be concealed in the shine. Forceps, please. Pull, chisel, cut, polish. There. Now that's what I call a smile. It's deadly!

OK. Is this a man or a woman? Would you check please, nurse? A woman? OK. Well. Flat may be good in Nebraska, but not in Beverly Hills. Silicon, please. Snip, push, stuff, sew. There we are. Wow! Those are good, I'm tempted to... Nurse, slap my hand, please. Thank you.

OK. Hips. Whoa. Cellulite city. Vacuum, please. Whoosh, suck, gurgle, spit. There. Looking slim, looking trim. OK. Ow! Varicose veins. Eeech! I hate those things. Hypo, please. Inject, inject, inject, swab. That ought to do it.

So what do you think, nurse? Oh what am I asking *you* for? Bob, what do you think? Great body, dog face huh? Yep! I do like a challenge. Scalpel.

OK, here goes. Snip, tuck, scrape, pull. Hack, chip, scoop, whittle, wax! Voila! Is that a face or is that a face?! Oh my God, I'm good. Bob? Damn right, she's ready for Prime time. You're all done, sweetheart. Now go out there and get your heart broken. Nurse, wheel her on out of here. Next!

Luck Be an Oscar Tonight

The tinsel town ladies sing this song
    Di-va, Di-va
Dresses so slinky and legs so long
    Oh Di-va Dey!
Trying to smile all night, couldn't get to sleep all day
I'll put my money on the bob-haired nag
Somebody bet on the gay.

When Film Stars Collide

Blimey! You damn Limey!
Said Arnold the Barbarian
Sucking in his gut

When a perturbed little
Mr. Bean accidentally farted
Inappropriately

At the prestigious awards ceremony
Attended by EVERYONE (who thought he was
Someone).

MEDIA MOGUL GENIUS

A murder was committed
how to understand the senselessness
the brutal act of this —
what?
who can interpret?
who to interview?
psychologists, sociologists, criminologists
people who study these kinds of
shall we call them — nutcases —
for a living?

No.

Let's talk to the neighbors, the co-workers, the gas station
    attendant
the former grade-school teachers who
really haven't got a clue, but who
cares
ordinary, everyday people
that's what makes great television!

(And sells all that high fructose corn syrup in Des Moines.)

Swallowing Goldfish

When the Corporation devoured
The television news
I no longer heard that
Sharp chatter, painful
Truthspeak that made it hard
To buy and sell
(without conscience)

But now I know

Nothing
I didn't know before
And somehow I believe
I know everything I need to know
To sleep soundly and dream
Impeccably
In black and white.

Pundits

You don't believe me
And I don't believe you
So is it any wonder
No one believes in anything
Anymore
Except muscles and lipstick
And botox and beer?

So you sell your product
And I'll sell mine
And may the best corporation
Win.

Ozzie and Harriet Got Cancelled

Ms. Harriet Nelson Jones is an Executive Director
No-nonsense boss
Wears a suit, plays golf and smokes cigars

Comes home to

Husband Bruce, unemployed welder
Wears an apron, cooks and
Cleans the dishes

Little Ricky, sweet 16
Watches TV
Plays video games and sometimes for fun

Builds pipe bombs off the Internet.

No Sunglasses

Look into my eye
What do you see?

Do you see the future
Do you see the past
Do you see the fire
Burning
Since the beginning of time?

Do you see the answer
Or the question
Do you see?
Do you understand?

Look carefully.

Look, before you cross the street.

If you don't look
You won't see
The truth barreling down
Without stopping.

Ozymandias II

Can you make me a name
Out of the clay of overused words
Make a sound that commands attention
In a cacophonous world that cannot
Distinguish
Its own music

Can it be that we are nothing more
Than an aboriginal dream
Once fitted to the life bone, now broken
Beneath the cosmic shoe of an
Inquisitional conquest

Leave me on the desert sand
An empty cup
A piece of bread
And a sharpened knife
To make the passage
From mirage to mirage

More interesting.

An Actor Prepared

An actor experiences
Other people's lives
Through a metamorphosis of mind

Words sifted through a membrane of
Archetypal truth

Emotion held in space and time
And passed from body to body
Becoming real and imagined

On stages of humanity
Bound together
In the fabric draped from
Shoulder
    to
        loin

Footfalls on a distant planet
Three orbits from the sun.

MISTER SUCCESSFUL MAN

Mr. Man, you are what we call successful.
We see your cars, we see your big house
We see your picture in the paper and on the TV
And we say, man, he's a mister, a Mister Man.
You wanted to make money and you did, man.
Oh mister, did you ever make money, oh man.
And that's why we say you are successful.

We just wish that we could be like you, Mr. Man —
Successful, with lots of money.
We want our picture in the paper and on the TV.
We want to spend most of our time playing golf, too.
But that's why you're a Mister Man and we're not.

We just didn't want the money bad enough, Mr. Man.
We wasted too much time watching our kids play baseball
And dress like turkeys in the school plays
And now we'll never be successful.
We'll just be ordinary Mr. and Mrs. So and So
With a broken-down car and a mortgage and —
Come to think of it, I never did much like playing golf
Anyway.

Hmm. That's interesting.

FACE-TO-FACE

My head was screwed-on sideways
So I only saw one face on my

Good friend Bobbo Lou who
Took one look at my gullibility

And cashed in with his other face
Before I had time to grow up.

Only in Vegas

Indiana drove up
Ford focused
Six-gun on the hip, ready
(Blushing Belle beside him)
Said
"You open?"

"You betcha, lover boy," the buxom matron answered.
"Whatcha got?"

He pulled out sixty big ones and laid 'em on her hand.

"Hang on to your holster. Be back in a sec."

She whisked through the portal
A pink and blue cabana —
Overhead the putti strummed their harps of gold
Stars twinkling with promise

"Howdy."
Said the stranger, dressed in black
"Name's Steve. Pastor Steve. Glad to meetcha."
"Do you take this woman, Blushing Belle
To be your lawfully wedded wife?"

I do. She do.

"I now pronounce you man and wife."

And how. He kissed the bride.
Threw that baby into gear and
Rode off into a neon sunset.

Down with the Ship

Someone (unnamed) bought the media pie
Oh my
Cut it into a minimum number of parts
And gave a succulent slice to each of his
Very best buddies.

Now they sit around on yachts
Smoking cigars and drinking
Swill
The whole world
Mindlessly going about
Their business

Unable to determine
Invisible truths of sunken treasure
Hidden in an ocean of

Lies.

MOVIE MAGIC

Movies
Reflect the way we'd like the world to be
Not the world that is
The slick beginning middle and end is so
Reassuringly tidy and complete
Serendipitous resolution
Premeditated script-ure according to some
Dollar-witted hackster wallowing in the
Oozing sentiment of
Popular culture and taste (less ness).

We willingly partake in the delusion
Believing in things that never were
People that don't exist
Times that clocks have never measured.

How ill-inspired we are when
Life, brawling in its crude matter-of-fact way
Decks us with the cold fist of reality
The shots never flattering, makeup that runs with
Sweat
Hair tousled out of place
Clothes that cannot be pressed
Ironed out so efficiently
Between takes.

DISNEYFIED

Denial
A beautiful Peter Pan dream of a place
Where you may never-never wake up.

Mouths of Babes

"I want to be famous,"
    she said.
Little 13-year-old pigtailed girl
Braces to force a smile.

Famous? For what?

"I don't know. Just famous.
I want to be the person
Everyone looks at
In all the magazines and on
TV."

"Do you want to be famous for doing something
Important?"

"I don't care.
Just as long as I ain't a nobody.
Like you."

When she sat back down
Her arms folded in defiance across her chest,
The world cringed.

CELLULOID LOVERS

She fell in love with his image
He fell in love with hers
When they went to bed
What magic!
A collision of stars
Passion played in the whip and tail of
Unrestrained fantasy.

When they woke up in the morning and
Looked into each other's eyes
They realized they'd been duped
Real people with real problems
How did that get in the script?

Santa Monica Pier

The evening drops like a veil
To hide the innocence of
Childhoods lost and never found
Popcorn and cotton candy
Buttery and bitter sweet

Red neck beach bangers hanging
Under the bridge
Chicks in line with tattooed thighs

A coaster's chilling thrill on the moonlit rails...

The stroll along the boards
Is more of a hustle
Knocking elbows through the crowds

Games of no chance played
With a shot in the pocket
Lips loosened for the chase
Denim ripped in the arid
Breeze, the ocean salt

Stinging the eyes without a clue.

The Envelope Please

Flash!
Bulb!
Limos leaping, breaching white whales
Waving in blast of briny foam
A sea of paramecia
Doors blow-holed open
Flash! Flash! Flash!
Swath of naked skin
Exposed
Garments slipping into fissure and crevice
Where mortals dare not go.

These are the chosen few.

Jewels dangling from occidental lobes
Busts as big as Burbank
Propped so primly for a
Pertinent view
Tuxes pressed on Toms and Jerrys
Bow-tie and wing-tip slick
Black and white no gray matter here
Or question sharp from media drones
To puncture
Airy notions.

No. The ropes hold back the mob.

The masquers of this sacred ball
Come
In divine right
With red carpet laid
To consummate and consecrate
In royal approbation
The progeny of power.

CELEBRITY WATCHING

Losers are much more interesting
(The real winners) who
Know what it is like to experience and

Suffer, the compassionate ones
Who recognize the sameness in
Difference, who cannot understand

Inhumanities wreaked upon
Innocents, silver-spooned notions of
Success, bulldozing through virgin

Forests, without the slightest
Consideration, or regard
Ground and sold into a

Cliff-top villa with a pool and
Sundeck overlooking
The ocean.

Silver Screen

We take a little man
Somewhat more appealing than the rest
Blow him up 50 feet high
His face as big as a storefront window
A towering Colossus to straddle
The straits of our inadequacy
Shoulders to carry our burden of failure
Champion of our dignity
Always honorable, never cheap
He makes us believe we are better than
We are

He fights when we need to fight
Feels when we need to feel
Thank God we never chance to meet him
Short and balding in the flesh, without make-up
Hear silly words, words that are his own
Not scripted out of myth
What a shock that would be

Why
We'd have to completely re-evaluate
Who we are
And what's worse
Uncomfortably disillusioned
Find something else to do on Friday nights
That doesn't require much
Thinking.

Bernhardt on her Knees

She was a brilliant actress
I'd seen her play Medea
But shy in nature, no beauty
To be sure, she wasn't
Visible to bean-counting
Suits munching sandwiches
In cramped audition rooms
Wielding cell phones like
Stilettos to spear a deal.

She could have been a star
A talent for the ages
But golden opportunity never came
In modest insecurity she
Toiled under hot lights
Making bland commercials
The homely housewife scrubbing
Floors.

Griffith Park Observatory

You can see it from
Some great distance
Far below
Looking up

A majestic dome
Commanding the promontory
High above the city
Gleaming white in the sun
Like a great robed prophet
Delivering truths to an
Unknowing world

You decide to make the journey
Up the winding hillside
Up, up, up
The anticipation mounting
But the cars begin to pile up
Bumper to bumper
Slowing your once steady advance
To a crawl
And the top, so close, seems
Oh so far
Away

Finally, you arrive
A parking lot chocked full of
People and steel, frustration and fumes
Car after car looking for that proverbial
Space

If only you weren't tied to this
Particular orbit, circling endlessly
The gravity of that building holding you
At arm's length, but no further
Till finally, you give up
Make your way back down the hill
From whence you came

Some other day perhaps
You'll come back and try again
And once again you'll be
Defeated

The quest is ongoing
The night forever young
And someday if you're lucky
You, too, may see the stars.

Close Call

I had a notion to take Hollywood to bed
But she was so consumed by

Veneer-real diseases
I politely backed out and said
Goodnight

For fear I might not live
To see the morning.

Who Killed the Fourth Estate?

You did.
You could have done something.
But you just sat there
Pretending life was something you
Didn't have to participate in.
All you did was sit and stare
Eating your greasy hamburgers and all-too-
American fries
Pretending it wasn't just a fattening junk food
For the brain.

Now it's too late.

The corpse is cold and blue.
Truth, that is.
Truth.
But you didn't really care anyway, did you?
Truth was such an annoyance.
Now we have plenty of Lies to kick back and
Relax with
Have a brew
And tell all those bullshit stories
We thought no one in their right mind

Would ever want to listen to.

Colorado Dreaming

The cabin
Set on Rocky Mountainside
Snow-capped peaks across the valley
Green meadow and wildflower below

Wood-burning fireplace
Logs piled high
Bacon sizzling on the skillet
Smoke curling through the pines

The dog barks
An echo rolls along the road
A bird in answer
Wings a song into the sky

L.A. is gone
A stone skipped upon a mountain stream
Washed into the sea
My boots crunch the needles in applause.

While Turning Off the Television

In the competing toss
of political winds
of right and left
and wrong and wrong
upside-down doers
making proclamations that have
no meaning, no substance
no form

We call this "democracy"

and use the word with a
cynical grin
the world exposed to its own
hypocrisy
the wasted lives of millions
struggling
without power
to be free.

Winners and Losers

As an outsider, looking in
You might wonder why
No glory, no golden global Oscar
Is bestowed on those
Who survive — quietly behind closed curtains
Rejected and defiled in
Swamps of Hollywood slime
Egos sucking blood out of
Dead turnips
The two, three, four, five, six-faced
Fiends fingering foul figures of
Obscene wealth

O why not those others
Those true believers be
Applauded

Their honor and dignity yet intact
Motives still pure
Unsullied by political machination
Why not these in any walk of life?
We might well ask the question.
Where are those survivors?
Can any pass through inner sanctums
Narrow corridors of gust and glitter
Without offering
In rites of filial obligation
Sacred sacrifice of
Heart and soul?

Does Anyone Remember?

No. The time is gone now.

The time when it was possible
To change the course
Of this all-too-human
History.

There is no one left now
To remember
No one, even, to care.

All the achievements of
And all that was noble about
Mankind
Long now – disappeared.

Nothing is left but
Ruin and rubble
A planet devastated
By selfishness, arrogance, and
Greed.

And all those little lives
Consumed with their petty
Contrivances
Now mean nothing.

Cancelled.

Like a reality show
That wasn't worth watching
In the first place.

The Hollywood Ending

is always upbeat
nothing depressing or upsetting
or unsettling to make living
even harder than it is

people won't pay money for that

so let's say you, dear reader, are the writer
now
look into the future and what
do you see?
for yourself, your children
your grandchildren?

the ending is up to you

good or bad, happy or sad
you've always been the creator
of your own destiny
haven't you?
so take courage and have at it!
but be sure to take off

your sunglasses

and really enjoy that spectacular sunset
before the credits roll —
the fleeting moment, after all
can never be recaptured.

ACKNOWLEDGEMENTS

Grateful acknowledgement is made to the editors and publishers of the following anthologies, periodicals and web journals in which poems in this collection first appeared, some in slightly different versions.

Apollo's Lyre, "Bernhardt on her Knees"
Apparent Depth, "Beverly Hills Billie"
Apples and Oranges, "A Supermodel in Bed"
Art Villa, "The Angel and the Devil"
CER*BER*US, "Hollywood Surgeon"
CommonSense2, "Marketing and Research"
Cotworld, "Do the Limbo"
Eklectique, "Game Show"
EWGPresents This Hard Wind, "Porn Star," "Silver Screen"
FusionInk, "Andy's Flagrant Moon"
The Hold, "The Face in the Tube"
The Inditer, "Disneyfied"
Kookamonga Square, "The Envelope Please," "Winners and Losers"
Lost Beat Poetry, "Who Wants to be an Idiot"
Nasty, "Santa Monica Pier," "The TV Executive"
Panic! Brixton Poetry, "Del Usion," "The Lost Works of Shakespeare"
Poetfest, "Colorado Dreaming"
Short North Gazette, "Sink Hole"
Stark Raving Sanity, "Gone Hollywood"
X-it Press, "Tee Vee"

About the Author

Laurence Overmire has had a multi-faceted career as writer, actor, director, educator, and genealogist. His award-winning poetry has been widely published in the U.S. and abroad in hundreds of journals, magazines and anthologies. Known to many for his weekly segments as poet-in-residence on The Jeff Farias Show, Overmire is an advocate for peace, justice, human and animal rights, and the environment. Though his work can be provocative in its direct confrontation of social issues, he continually underscores the need for understanding and compassion in the world.

Overmire began his professional acting career at the world-renowned Guthrie Theatre in Minneapolis. After a season working with some of the finest stage directors of the time – Alan Schneider, Richard Foreman, Liviu Ciulei, Garland Wright – he moved to New York performing in several Off-Broadway productions including *Don Juan* at the New York Shakespeare Festival in Central Park as well as on Broadway in *Amadeus* starring Frank Langella and Mark Hamill. He also performed in numerous regional theatres across the country and landed various roles on the television soaps, ranging from a priest on *All My Children* to a homicidal maniac on *Loving*.

To broaden his acting opportunities, like so many others before him, Overmire decided to move to the west coast and give Hollywood a shot. Those experiences form the basis of this book.

Gradually, he found his interests shifting away from acting and toward other pursuits. He met the love of his life, Nancy McDonald, and together they founded *The Writer's Lab,* a non-profit organization to promote quality writing in the entertainment industry.

In 1994, the Northridge Earthquake struck. Laurence and Nancy felt fortunate to have survived - the houses of their neighbors plunged down the Hollywood hillside. Soon it became clear to Laurence that poets and Hollywood weren't all that compatible. He and Nancy got hitched in Vegas and embarked upon a new life together. Today, they can be found reveling in the wilds of Oregon, living life to its fullest and enjoying the sunsets.

www.ingramcontent.com/pod-product-compliance
Lightning Source LLC
Chambersburg PA
CBHW070101100426
42743CB00012B/2617